UNLEASHING YOUR INNER WEIRDO:

A JOURNEY TO AUTHENTIC LEADERSHIP

ALAN MARSHALL II

DEDICATION

To my wife Ashley, who encourages me through difficult seasons and continues to love me unconditionally. To my parents, who taught me to stand up for what I believe in. To my three children, Aria, Alan, and Amani, who bless me each day with their beautiful and unique personalities. To Pastors Paul and Donna Hylton, who lead by example and push me to be the best version of myself possible. To Kay Randall for mothering me in the Gospel and Stephen Randall for always being a voice of reason. Finally, to my close friends and mentors, Wai-Yee Schmidt, Rev. Debra Hopkins, and Glenn Russo, thank you for giving me a shot at greatness and steering me toward my destiny.

CONTENTS

PREFACE

Whether we realize it or not, each of us is engaged in a raging battle within ourselves. This battle isn't physical but internal; it's the war for authenticity. In a world filled with media spins, false information, scams, propaganda, celebrity narratives, and political spiels, discerning what's real from what's fake has become increasingly challenging.

As modern technology advances, it's become commonplace for social media users to showcase only the highlights of their lives while downplaying the struggles and turbulence it took to achieve success. Moreover, many are inclined to flaunt extravagant lifestyles, with private jet flights, luxurious mansions, and lavish parties, only to be exposed later when it's revealed that these displays were staged or exaggerated.

Rather than solely addressing society's obsession with valuing falsehoods, I'd like this book to focus on the inner conflict that drives many into a race to maintain facades in order to impress others. This internal battle, I've discovered, is the most formidable.

This book isn't about assigning blame or pointing fingers; it's about acknowledging the hidden, silent battles we all endure. It's about shedding the masks we wear and embracing our authentic selves. The 'weirdo' within, the one who doesn't neatly fit into predefined categories, often harbors our most genuine and profound leadership qualities.

If you've ever felt like an outsider or hidden your quirks and unique gifts, this book is for you. It's a call to step into the light that God has given you, to lead authentically, and to showcase your unique, God-given gifts. As you journey through each chapter of this book, my hope is that you'll experience a revelation of what it truly means to be a uniquely designed instrument of God.

SECTION I:

THE ROOT, THE SOURCE, AND THE LIFESTYLE

ONE
DEEPLY ROOTED

WHO AM I?

"For you formed my inward parts; you knitted me together in my mother's womb. I praise you, for I am fearfully and wonderfully made. Wonderful are your works; my soul knows it very well."
(*Psalms 139:13-14 ESV*)

As a child, I often found myself at the center of attention. To this day, I am unsure if being in the spotlight was due to my intense curiosity for life or a deep hunger to express what was in my heart. Either way, I was always front and center, and the result of my fifteen minutes of fame would usually result in a glorious celebration or a painful lesson in the form of rejection.

For three generations, both sides of my family served as members of an organization called Jehovah's Witnesses. Most of my days were spent hanging around people from the organization we called friends, sometimes even family. There was a closeness that I was not only fond of but deeply proud to proclaim. For us, the pride of being a Jehovah's Witness came with a sense of style, fervor for evangelism, and consistent attendance at the Kingdom Hall three times a week.

From age five, I gave small sermonettes called talks in the Theocratic Ministry School, a training ground that prepared the congregants for door-to-door ministry and public speaking. My earliest memories often involved speaking in front of crowds, standing up for my beliefs at school, missing holiday parties, and even being teased about being a Jehovah's Witness by classmates. While the bullying at times was intense, I believe that my upbringing made me stronger and more resilient as a person.

On my twenty-first birthday, I attended a party for an African dance reunion when I was struck by two things that seemed to be diametrically opposed. The first was a birthday cake being presented in my honor, and the second was my future wife Ashley arriving at the party. I didn't know where to focus. I didn't celebrate my birthday and surely did not want a cake, but my jaw nearly dropped as I saw the woman of my dreams.

About a week later, we began to date, and over the next year, we would find ourselves deeply in love but fighting about one critical issue. She was a Christian, and I was a Jehovah's Witness studying to be baptized. What I find most interesting about this time in life is that she never tried to convert me, even in our most intense theological arguments. What struck me about her was her passion for God and how she lived her life privately and publicly. For Ashley, there was no difference, and I admired her consistency.

After a year of dating, I was told that my desire to officially become a Jehovah's Witness through baptism would not be fulfilled. As I sat with the elders, I was questioned about dating an "unbeliever." I was told that our relationship meant that I was unequally yoked, and because of this, I was disqualified from baptism.

That night, I called Ashley in tears. My heart felt like it was ripped in pieces as I told her that we needed to end our relationship. I explained to her that my dedication to God needed to be stronger than my dedication to her. Hearing this, she cried but understood what needed to be done and was willing to end the relationship for the sake of my faith. For some reason, we ended the conversation without officially breaking up.

After our conversation, I ran to the most secluded space in my apartment, which was a large pantry I had converted into a recording studio. I sat on the floor clutching my knees in the fetal position, and as the tears ran down my face, I told God: "If this is where you want me to be, then keep me here, but if it's not, take me wherever you want me to go, and I'll go."

A year passed, and I made several attempts to go back to the Kingdom Hall, but every time I walked through the door, my stomach felt as if someone had practiced tying knots with my intestines. So instead, I stayed home, read the New World Translation Bible, and prayed as I had been taught.

On one occasion, Ashley came to my house during a break from school. She told me that she was going to sing at church and asked me if I would come to see her. Immediately, my mind raced to tell her no, but for some reason, I opened my mouth to speak, and the word yes came out of it. I wanted to rescind my decision as fast as possible, but I kept hearing the words of Matthew 5:37 playing repetitively in my head. "Let your yes mean yes, and your no mean no. (Matthew 5:37 CEB)

I rode to the church nervously with Ashley's parents. If I recall correctly, Ashley's dad made a joke, and my laughter sliced through some of my nervousness. As we stepped through the doors of the sanctuary, my nerves settled as I was greeted by an elderly Hispanic woman affectionately named Sister Emma. She kissed me on the cheek and hugged me like she knew me. It was strange, but just about everyone greeted me this way. Little did I know that they had already been praying for me once they found out Ashley had been dating a Jehovah's Witness. I didn't know what to make of this small non-denominational church with Pentecostal roots, but it felt right. I felt at home.

When Ashley returned to school the next week, I called her mother and requested that she bring me every week. I attended Bible studies, Sunday services, worship practices, and even the Christmas cantata. I was so intrigued and hungry for the Bible that I read through the New Testament in just a few months. I wanted everything I could get my hands on that involved Jesus.

It was at the Christmas cantata that I made a decision that sent shockwaves throughout my entire family. I decided to give my life to Christ. If I am being honest, I wasn't moved by the beautiful production or swayed by deep emotion. What I felt was the tangible embrace of the Holy Spirit. The embrace made me feel like someone wrapped a warm blanket around my soul. I turned to Ashley and said, "I think Jesus just hugged me." She snickered as if she knew the feeling but continued to let the Lord work through me.

Weeks later, I mustered up the courage to speak to my parents. I had so many questions for them as my newfound faith caused me to see my life as a Jehovah's Witness in a different light. As I spoke to my mother and father, I expressed many things out of a place of deep hurt, and so did they. The child who was once a bold proclaimer of their faith had turned his back on the organization. For years, I heard about a man who left and became a preacher. The thought of doing such a thing was shunned and viewed as heretical. I was now the black sheep, and my decision to follow Christ made my entire family cringe.

As I think about the verbal sparring matches I had with well-meaning people, the fights I had with family members, and the distance that caused me to feel like an outcast among friends I had known my entire life, I realize that this was the inception of my journey to authenticity. A journey paved with life lessons that shaped me as a leader.

While facing rejection from the life I was leaving, I found solace in the development I was getting from the Church. To be completely honest, I often look back and stand amazed at how God provided such a dynamic environment for me to grow as a new Christian. Still, the pressure to fit the mold of pastoral ministry loomed ominously in the background, and people filled with the best of intentions guided me to look and act like the quintessential pastor. Despite the accolades, degrees, and compliments from people suggesting I take on the role of a pastor, pastoring will always be something I do, but it will never equate to who I am.

God's Plot Twist

Let me share with you a moment that turned my world upside down. Picture this: I'm sitting at the edge of my bed in the middle of the day, and suddenly, I'm caught up in what I can only describe as a vision from God. It was like being awake in a dream, where everything felt real and tangible, yet I was watching a narrative unfold before me. I was caught up in a divine dialogue, a revelation of a path laid out for me that challenged everything I knew about my life.

As I sat at the edge of my bed, I was completely engrossed in the vision, God showed me three square tubes, like television screens, each one revealing a different way He would use me across the globe. The first screen was exhilarating. In this vision, I was traveling the world, setting up churches, mentoring leaders, and speaking to large congregations. It was everything I ever wanted, or so I thought. But then God asked me, "Is this what you want?" I responded, "Absolutely, this is the dream!" But then He said something that hit me hard: "You'll have less impact doing this than what I'm about to show you next."

Can you imagine the anticipation? The next screen showed me preaching to stadiums filled with hundreds of thousands of people. I was thinking, "This is it. This has to be the reason for my calling." But again, God surprised me, saying, "You'll have less impact here than on the next screen." At this point, I'm baffled. I had been gearing up for ministry for the last ten years by studying theology, pastoral care, and polishing my sermons. What could possibly top that?

Then, the last screen. What I saw was so out of left field it floored me. It was a vision of me bridging the worlds of ministry and business, advising leaders in both spheres globally. But here's the kicker. What God was showing me was entirely out of my comfort zone.

So, here's the big question. What do you do when God's vision for your life crashes into your own? I always thought of myself as a person who would dive headfirst to take on a challenge, but in this instance, I was terrified. This revelation of how I would fulfill my purpose scared me to the core. Despite the fear, I knew I had to follow this path, even though, if I'm being honest, I did so reluctantly because my self-perception was at war with this new calling from God.

Let's talk about the tension between who we think we are, who God calls us to be, and the leap of faith it takes to step into the unknown. The unknown is where we find our true purpose. It's not in the safety of the familiar, but in the wild, sometimes intimidating, freedom of God's grand design for our lives. The reality of this life-startling revelation was that it was outright weird. I had no experience consulting, let alone leading pastoral leaders on an international scale. Whatever God would do in my life would have to be by a divine design.

Answering the 'Why' of Self-Identity

Embarking on the journey of self-discovery often begins with a seemingly simple question: "Who am I?" It's a question many of us have pondered at some point in our lives. But more often than not, the answers we come up with barely scratch the surface of understanding our true selves. Some may respond by answering the question with their job titles, while others might define themselves by their relationship roles. While these descriptions may be accurate, they do not encompass the depth of who we are as individuals. So, let's shift the paradigm. Instead of asking, "Who am I?" Try pondering, "Why am I?"

Have you ever wondered about the root of your being? Considered the experiences, relationships, spiritual moments, challenges, inspirations, and family ties that have sculpted your worldview? I recall a moment from a Netflix documentary featuring Tony Robbins. He was counseling a successful woman grappling with the shadow of her difficult upbringing. As she spoke of the contrasting influences of her nurturing mother and abusive father, Robbins offered her a perspective shift. He highlighted the strength and resilience she'd gained from her adversities. It was a transformative moment, illustrating the power of reframing our experiences and understanding their impact on our identities.

For this young woman, confronting her way of thinking allowed her to experience freedom from a debilitating mindset. A mindset that allowed her to be successful externally but broken internally. To truly grasp who you are and begin a change process, it's vital first to understand the 'why,' 'what,' and 'how' that often hides beneath the surface of your decisions, actions, and results.

The Triad of Authentic Leadership

Every aspiring leader venturing into authentic leadership should ask three pivotal questions: 'Why,' 'What,' and 'How?' These questions form a triad for authentic leadership and success. With these insights in hand, an aspiring leader is well-equipped to craft a path that is true to themselves and resonant with the needs of those they aim to inspire and lead.

Why?

The question 'why' causes you to dive deep into your belief systems and perceptions. And perception is at the heart of decision-making, influencing our thoughts, actions, and the paths that we choose. The 'why' delves into one's core beliefs and values, sculpted by upbringing, education, societal norms, culture, and religious tenets. Understanding your 'why' in life allows you to understand your motivations and the rationale behind your choices.

Imagine a garden infested with weeds. Those familiar with gardening understand the menace that weeds pose. They deplete resources, overshadowing other plants. The reality is that unless uprooted entirely, weeds resurge. This garden is a metaphor for our lives, where weeds symbolize negative beliefs and insecurities. If left unchecked, they overshadow our potential. The 'why' enables us to identify and address the root of these deep-seated beliefs, ensuring they don't dictate our future actions.

If you are trapped in a cycle of detrimental behaviors affecting personal and professional relationships, it's time to introspect. Look beyond the behavior and delve into the belief systems and structures steering your actions.

What?

Now that we have addressed the 'why,' let's deal with 'what' and the 'how' as they are closely connected. As a consultant and a minister, I have spent much time counseling people with enormous potential. More often than not, they are strongly convicted people with great vision for their future and the future of others. Yet, they are just as often people who fail at implementing their convictions and vision in their own lives. While the question of 'why' addresses core principles and deeply held beliefs, the question of 'what' addresses action. When you are assured of your core ideals and beliefs, the follow-up question should be, what will I do about them?

Despite what you believe is a core principle in life, there is a strong correlation between actions and results. In essence, what you do affects how things will turn out. You could deeply believe that you have the figure of a Sports Illustrated swimsuit model or a championship bodybuilder. Still, if you stay out of the gym and eat fast food daily, chances are that your ambitions will not likely become a reality.

When a person understands who they are, it becomes the framework for what they do. If your core value is to live a healthy life at peak fitness, you will set disciplines that cause you to live a lifestyle promoting health, wellness, and athleticism. Ultimately, engaging in a disciplined lifestyle allows you to sync your core values and actions in a way that leads to better results.

How?

The final question in this triad for authentic leadership dives into "how." 'How' directly relates to the results of an action. Knowing 'why' and 'what' is only half the battle. When a person takes the time to examine the results and reasons behind their actions, they begin a process known as looped learning. Now, I realize that going into a deep and complex explanation of single and double-looped learning may cause some to glaze over while reading, so instead, let's talk about it at a basic level.

In single and double-looped learning, there are three steps that form the foundation of decision-making. The first step is a governing principle or a reason behind wanting to take an action. The next step is an action that implements what a person believes, and the final step is the result that an action produces.

In the case of single-looped learning, a person's results, whether good or bad, lead them to take another action rather than going back to their reason for starting the first place. You might ask what is so wrong with 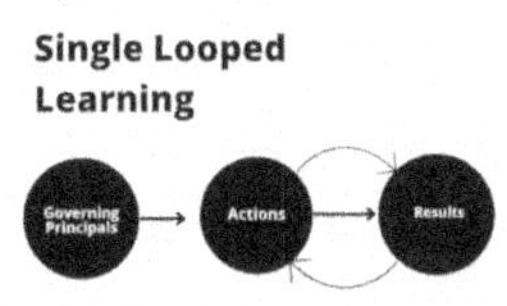

Single Looped Learning

this style of learning. Well, we have all heard Albert Einstein's definition of insanity, right? If not, it is a person (or an organization) that does the same thing repetitively and expects different results. This is the case with single-loop learners. They fail to reanalyze the governing principles for which their actions and results produce. In turn, they end up living a life that happens to them rather than living an intentional life that happens for them.

On the contrary, double-looped learning, which I advocate as the better model for living, is a recipe for successful authentic leadership. This style of learning highlights the governing principle as the 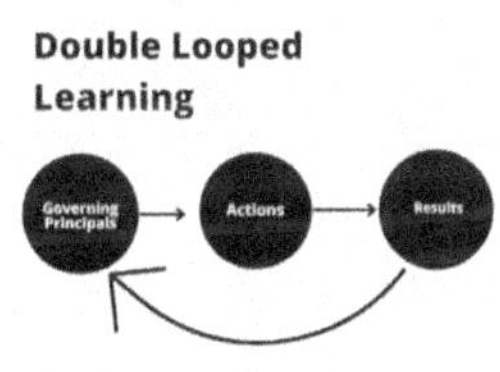

Double Looped Learning

framework for decision-making. When you take the time needed to reanalyze the 'why' before you move into the 'what,' and 'how,' you are far more likely to take more effective actions and produce better results for yourself and the people you are called to serve.

You can begin today to embrace learning and reflection by going beyond the surface of your actions. This involves questioning your core beliefs and principles after experiencing the outcomes of your actions. Authentic leadership requires this transformative journey, which promotes growth and ensures that your actions align with your true purpose and values. By engaging in self-reflection, leaders can make well-informed decisions that produce meaningful and effective outcomes for themselves and those they lead. This commitment to intentional leadership creates an environment where genuine vision can thrive and impact the world around them.

Conclusion

Do you remember the vision from the beginning of this chapter? About nine months after this encounter with God, I was deeply entrenched in a one-hundred-million-dollar land development deal. I wasn't looking for such an opportunity. I was still trying to get over the idea that my preconceived idea of ministry wouldn't be my next step.

I was deeply considering how God's plan would unfold in my life when a gentleman from a prominent company approached me. He requested that I pitch his residential apartment development to a local city. It is important to understand that at this time, I had no political or land development experience, but I did have a lifetime of public speaking experience and a strong capacity to learn, so I accepted.

My lack of experience did not deter the gentleman from offering me the opportunity. Instead, he took the time to teach me. Over three weeks, he taught me everything I needed to know about the project, navigating city meetings and developing and maintaining relationships with local businesses and politicians.

Little did I know that in our initial conversation, the Spirit of God would lead me to suggest shifting the development from being stalled in city meetings to being passed unanimously. Nor did I realize that I would be used to design a historic program that would provide equity and justice for contractors working on the development. Today, I am blessed to consult for his secular and Christian organizations that develop property and plant thousands of churches worldwide.

Making the differentiation between what I do and who I am has been critical to my journey as an authentic leader. I can't help but ponder the countless amounts of people who are steered to fit the mold of patterns that cause them to miss out on what God would ordain for their lives. As you move forward in your journey, I implore you to be introspective. Take a deep dive into the reasons why you think, act, and behave the way you do. Look closely at your actions and how they play out in your everyday life, and then see if the results fit where you feel you are destined to be. When you do this, you avoid wasting time on distractions, and you grow closer to unleashing the authentic leader inside of you.

TWO
TAPPING INTO THE SOURCE

"I am the vine; you are the branches. If you remain in me and I in you, you will bear much fruit; apart from me, you can do nothing.
(John 15:5 NIV)

Have you ever questioned what it means to be authentic? Depending on who you ask, you will likely get varying answers. Some define authenticity as keeping it real or being transparent about their feelings and emotions. But let's face it, there is a time and a place to wear your emotions on your sleeve. A person who displays their emotions in a non-tactful, unempathetic, and inappropriate way is considered emotionally unintelligent.

Others have defined leading with authenticity as someone acting upon their core beliefs. This also poses an issue as history has painted the gruesome picture of crusaders, jihadists, and criminals who acted upon their most sincere convictions. While both definitions capture aspects of authenticity, they fail to reach the heart of the matter. The reality is that when we speak of authentic leadership, we often circle the very core of what drives true authenticity. It's not just about being genuine or transparent, but it's about tapping into the source that solidifies the nature of our identity and purpose.

For the Christian leader, the foundational source of authenticity is found only in Christ. Out of a place of deep intimacy with Jesus, the momentum to move authentically throughout life is established. The Bible declares, "For in Him we live, move, and have our being. (Acts 17:28 ESV) This means that life, movement, and our very existence is sustained only by God. Contrary to what many believe, pursuing education, healthy living, and philanthropy are only supplemental to a successful life. Tapping into the source to live and lead with authenticity is a constant acknowledgment that who we are is not determined by awards and accolades, nor by our most sincere convictions. It is determined by how closely we learn to abide in the presence of God.

As humans, the ability to connect and live a life guided by our Creator is nothing short of a miracle. When we allow Christ to inform and shape our leadership, we plug into a more powerful, resourceful, efficient, and intelligent source than anything we can come up with on our own. The writer of Psalm 42 uses the following phrase to depict our connection with God, "Deep calleth unto deep at the noise of thy waterspouts: all thy waves and thy billows have gone over me." (Psalm 42:7 KJV) The word "waterspout" can be translated as waterfall or water tunnel in its original translation. One of the only times we can see heaven's depth meet the earth's depth is when a cyclone or "water tunnel" is spinning over the ocean. When our souls are surrendered to God, the depth of our mind, will, and emotions connect to

God's heart, hands, and mouth, allowing us to lead from a place that is indeed miraculous.

The Miracle of Authentic Leadership

The miracle of authentic leadership is that there is a pattern throughout the Bible of God using people considered unqualified to accomplish extraordinary feats. When the testimonies of the great men and women of God are examined further, it is interesting to see how God takes the skills that often appear irrelevant and uses them to accomplish the miraculous.

Once a shepherd, David used the same slingshot that protected his father's sheep from predators to conquer a giant threatening the Israelites. Sampson's cunning personality helped deceive the Philistines, leading to their downfall. The widow of Zarephath turned her limited resources into a sustaining miracle during a drought, and Apostle Peter's sense of boldness, which sometimes earned Jesus's rebuke, led him to perform countless miracles in the New Testament. In these stories, we see a pattern: God harnesses our inherent traits to mold us into leaders fulfilling His divine plan.

One can look no further than Jesus choosing uneducated fishermen, tax collectors, and political assassins to be the leaders of the first-century church. As Christian leaders, we have often heard and used the saying, "God does not call the qualified but qualifies the called?" This couldn't be truer for the lives of the biblical characters that operate in miraculous feats. For instance, Moses, who later confidently led his people out of Egypt and parted the Red Sea, was hesitant and uncertain, questioning his abilities at the burning bush.

When we examine the confrontation between God and Moses at the burning bush, we see what it looks like to lead authentically with God as the source of our leadership. At the burning bush, Moses questioned who he was, what he should say, his authority, and how it would be received. At every question posed by Moses, God answered in such a way that would suggest that Moses was simply a vessel being used to accomplish God's will on the earth. When Moses asks God his name, the Lord replies: "I AM WHO I AM," (YHWH) which can also be interpreted as "to cause to become." God takes the unlikely, peculiar, and outright weirdos like you and me and causes us to be leaders who operate powerfully.

The authentic leader understands that "man looks on the outward appearance, but the Lord looks on the heart." (1 Samuel 16:7 ESV). This means that your skill level is only a by-product of your obedience to your calling in Christ. To truly exist as an authentic leader, you must delve beyond identifying traits typically celebrated as leadership and position yourself to identify with the source from which authenticity flows. Only when we are submitted and conformed to Christ's image can we experience the miracle of authentic leadership.

Leading in Your Grace Bubble

Now that we have examined the miracle of authentic leadership, it is important to understand the role that grace plays in the life of a leader. If you have ever sat through a sermon on the topic of grace, you may have heard it defined as the unmerited favor of God. While this is an accurate definition, I would like to challenge you to accompany your understanding of grace as the enabling ability to accomplish what God has intended for you.

Combining these ideas, grace can be seen as God's favor, showcased through someone who might not seem deserving, enabling them to fulfill His will in unimaginable ways. This means that every individual possesses a unique form of grace. Think of it as having a personal "grace bubble." When we function within this bubble, we can achieve incredible feats that might seem difficult for others. But, if we step outside this bubble, we risk burnout, discredited authority, and compromised authenticity.

As of this writing, I'm a father to three, a husband, a clergy member, a consultant, a mentor, a musician, and an entrepreneur. I also hold several positions on various boards and committees in my town. To some, managing all these roles might sound overwhelming. You might wonder, "How does he manage everything?" All the roles I've listed fall within the grace bubble God granted me for this phase of my life.

The concept of a grace bubble revolves around the idea that each person harnesses different levels of grace for different times and seasons. Some graces last a lifetime, while others are temporary. For instance, I will forever be a father and a husband, but there may be periods when my role and responsibilities change. It's crucial to recognize that there might be phases when God pushes you to progress quickly and other times when He guides you to take things slower. Take Moses as an example. In one phase of his life, he was the prince of Egypt. Later, he found himself fleeing and taking refuge in the wilderness. In another stage, he brought plagues upon Egypt under God's command, and afterward, he spent time wandering in the desert. Each of these phases required a different operation of grace in the life of Moses.

Every Christian seeking to lead authentically should ponder three questions related to their grace bubble:

1. What are the areas and giftings of leadership that God has issued as a grace in my life?
2. How does God differentiate the graces in my life that are seasonal from the ones that are lifelong?
3. In what ways does God's grace make the most impact through me in the lives of others?

I suggest partnering with God to answer these questions as a foundation for discovering how to better operate in your grace bubble.

Surrender Your Day

A few years back, I embarked on a mission. In a rush, through the aisles of Hobby Lobby, I searched for scripture decals to put on the walls of my daughter's nursery. It wasn't about adding decoration but imparting an enduring lesson she would see as she grew up. I chose Psalms 46:10, "Be still and know that I am God."

In our world, we are constantly bombarded by a whirlwind of activities. We often get so caught up in our routines that taking a moment to listen to the Lord becomes an afterthought. Through my experiences and travels both within my country and abroad, I have noticed one common issue: the noise and complexity surrounding our everyday lives often hinder our ability to hear from God.

Hearing God is not much about factors such as being

gifted or specially chosen, but surrendering our day to the One who leads us better than we can lead ourselves. Amidst the chaos, I have trained myself to set aside distractions and attune myself to His voice. The level of our ability to push out distractions and focus on Christ determines how we will receive His message. With practice, His voice becomes increasingly distinct.

A powerful portrayal of this principle can be seen in the movie Selma regarding the pressure on Martin Luther King Jr. as he led a crowd across the Edmund Pettus Bridge. He stood before the masses of protestors on one side who pushed for him to advance toward Klan members and police who were intent on brutalizing them when they reached the other side of the Bridge; however, in a moment filled with anticipation, he paused to offer a prayer. In that stillness amidst all the chaos around him, he found guidance. Surprisingly, his decision to lead the marchers back without crossing the bridge may have been an intervention that saved lives.

It is crucial to understand that simply being still is not enough. It is through immersing ourselves in the presence of God that our connection deepens. My father and I share the same name, Alan. No matter our situation, whenever my mother called out our name, her tone made it clear who she was addressing. Our proximity and relationship with her sharpened our awareness of the tone of her voice.

Similarly, by engaging with God through prayer, meditation, reflection, Bible study, or bonding moments, we sharpen our spiritual understanding and sensitivity to His voice. It's a journey where we learn to recognize His voice and understand His guidance. The key lies in listening, practicing regularly, and embracing His presence.

Conclusion

Authenticity isn't merely about transparency or acting on conviction alone. It's about anchoring ourselves to the source of our identity and purpose. For us, as Christian leaders, that source is found in Christ. It's in Him that we discover the strength to lead with genuine authenticity, to be vessels for His will, reflecting His heart in every action we take.

The true miracle of leadership is not found in qualifications or expertise but in God's ability to use our unique traits, even those the world may deem insignificant, for His extraordinary purposes. It's understanding that God doesn't just call the equipped; He equips those He calls. As we learn to operate within our 'grace bubble,' recognizing God's divine empowerment for different seasons of our lives, we tap into the fullness of God's intention for us.

I encourage you to consider deeply the areas where God's grace is at work in your life. Discern the seasonal from the lifelong and seek to understand how this grace impacts those around you. As we do this, let's not forget to surrender each day to God. In the stillness, away from the world's noise, we find clarity and guidance from the One who knows us best.

Just as I chose Psalm 46:10 for my daughter's nursery wall, I urge you to 'Be still and know.' This means recognizing God's sovereignty in our busy lives. In this stillness, we hear His voice most clearly, guiding us towards authentic leadership. And like Dr. Martin Luther King Jr. at the Edmund Pettus Bridge, may we find the courage to be still, pray, and listen for that guidance, even when the weight of leadership rests heavily upon us.

In embracing His presence daily, we sharpen our

spiritual ears to His voice, just as we recognize the voice of someone we love. In this deep communion with God, we find the essence of truly authentic leadership. Step forward confidently, knowing that as we remain rooted in Christ, our leadership will be authentic, divinely inspired, and empowered. I pray that you begin to walk in the fullness of your calling with an authenticity that shines brightly for all to see.

THREE
THE ASSASSINATION OF AN AUTHENTIC LIFESTYLE

"God opposes the proud but gives grace to the humble." (James 4:6 ESV)

An alarm awakened me. The sound of my radio blasted violently, disturbing me enough to rattle me out of bed. My heart raced as if it would beat out of my chest, and despite the shock and awe of being jarred by the tones rifling through my ears, there was a loud and clear message. A carbon monoxide detector had been tripped, and a response was needed. It's been so long since my days as a volunteer firefighter that I can barely remember if I grabbed the fire engine to respond to the call or if I was off duty and left my radio on. Whatever the case, I knew that carbon monoxide was a silent killer and that without knowing its signs or having the right technology, it is undetectable and deadly.

Much like carbon monoxide, there is a silent killer that, if left without the proper balance, has the potential to take down the strongest leaders and cripple their authenticity. This assassin is a five-letter word called pride and strangles its opponents with weapons that are not always noticeable to the person in which they operate.

One way to discern whether pride has a hold on your life is to examine how you perceive yourself. Pride manifests when individuals regard themselves as occupying a position or status they do not genuinely hold. It is a mindset characterized by self-conceit, arrogance, or even feigned humility, frequently accompanied by self-deception. Pride can be observed in the child of a successful person who believes their accomplishments are solely due to their parents' achievements. It can be found in people who consider themselves slightly more clever, strategic, wise, superior, or conversely, less worthy than others. While these facets of pride are often evident to observers, they can remain silent to those ensnared by its grip.

In this chapter, I will explore two ways in which pride undermines the authenticity of leaders. The first method occurs when leaders allow a place for mediocrity, while the second involves the nurturing of a savior complex.

The Pride of Mediocrity

One of the passions closest to my heart is the art of public speaking. Growing up as a Jehovah's Witness, I was uniquely comfortable standing before large crowds to deliver a message. Every month, I would be tasked to deliver a five-minute sermon before a congregation of around 200 people. These sermons typically consisted of an introduction, a verbatim scripture reading in the body, a conclusion, and a public evaluation that the entire congregation would hear. While the idea of speaking publicly in such a manner might terrify many, for me, it felt as natural as breathing.

As I fast forward into my years as a young adult handling preaching assignments, I recall being invited to minister at services in different churches where multiple preachers were involved. In the African American church, events like the "seven last words" or the "five 'I Am' statements of Jesus" are what I'd like to call the "preaching Olympics." The format was consistent: each preacher received a statement from a biblical narrative, had a five-minute window to elaborate on it, and was expected to deliver a powerful message within that timeframe.

In practice, most preachers would extend their sermons to ten minutes or more, so the services often stretched on for hours. These situations became nerve-wracking, especially when I wasn't scheduled to preach last. Going second to last or anywhere in between meant I had to deliver either a passionate sermon that could be difficult for the preacher following me to match or intentionally speak in a more mediocre manner to avoid overshadowing the next speaker.

Let's stop momentarily and address the elephant in the room: the pride associated with my desire to please people. This pride blinded me to the true purpose of my preaching, which was meant to glorify Jesus, not myself.

In essence, pride is synonymous with insecurity, which can lead us to mediocrity. It is crucial to understand that compromising our God-given potential to seek the approval of others is a disservice to our divine calling and destiny in Christ. The Bible reminds us in Matthew 5:16 that our unique gifts and talents are meant to shine in a way that brings glory to God. When we diminish our gifts to gain the approval of others, we not only lose our authenticity but also leave behind a legacy of mediocrity for others to follow.

So, how do we navigate the challenge of letting our light shine or dimming it to fit in? The answer is clear: don't hold back; let it shine! As a leader, I can affirm that two atmospheres are contagious to followers: mediocrity and excellence. When we set a standard of excellence, others are drawn to it, seeking to engage and reach a higher level in their endeavors; however, when leaders create a culture of mediocrity, it affects them and marginalizes the talented individuals around them. Instead of setting a standard of excellence that would cause people to aspire towards a higher level of success, the culture of mediocrity rewards those who perform at subpar levels and further alienates those who are talented.

If you struggle with mediocrity as a leader, you must become aware of the insecurities fueling the behavior, causing you to underperform. Performing this analysis is critical, as mediocrity results from an insecure mindset. To start the change process and shift toward excellence, you must examine the cause of your insecurity and take steps to uproot it. You can start this process by asking God to reveal the root of your insecurities. Once He reveals them to you take the time to surrender them by confessing, repenting, and renouncing the belief or ideologies that have caused you to feel insecure. In addition to prayer, seek a licensed Christian counselor that can help you to walk in freedom.

The Savior Complex

The story of a hero has dominated entertainment for generations. Let's face it, everyone loves the idea of good triumphing over evil, especially when the bad guy is close to winning. The stories of heroic acts and extreme examples of bravery captivated my imagination and gave me hope that one day, I could help others in similar capacities. The only problem with this mentality is that it almost killed me and destroyed everything I loved.

At the height of the pandemic, I found myself in an unconscious rhythm of performance. Each day felt like a gauntlet of tasks that played out like a beautifully composed symphony for the deaf. That is, a symphony filled with the mannerisms of intense violin strokes, the pounding of drums, and the waving arms of a skilled conductor, but little to none of its intended effect on the hearing. These days, I was immersed in business dealings, international ministry meetings on Zoom, counseling sessions, pastorally caring for a campus without a chaplain, and helping friends, family, and loved ones. Notice closely that there was no mention of my wife or children or time dedicated to being spent with God. The result was that my health was failing. I was diagnosed as being prediabetic, having high cholesterol, high blood pressure, and having an anxiety disorder, and believe it or not, this was just the start of my problems.

Ultimately, all my problems came rushing to the spotlight as I found myself in tears in my daughter's nursery, confessing my struggles to my pastor and repenting before God. Only after this did I realize that what I was struggling with was a savior complex and that the remedy to fix it was to break the mentality that I was the answer to everyone else's problems.

The first step in addressing a savior complex is to define it. A savior complex is a psychological concept involving a person's strong desire to rescue others, frequently at the expense of their well-being. It is a behavioral pattern that typically originates from a sense of empathy, but if not properly managed, it can give rise to problems within relationships and cause personal hardship.

This complex is evident when leaders fail to set appropriate boundaries for themselves and their followers. A leader must realize that empathy is a double-edged sword that has the potential to boost or cripple authenticity. Authentic leadership without empathy is a style of leadership that is selfishly motivated. On the contrary, too much empathy can cause a leader to place themselves in compromising positions to fulfill the needs of others. Consider the male counselor rushing to meet the needs of a female patient in an intimate setting or a manager bending the rules to cover for a worker who is underperforming. In these instances, unchecked empathy drove the person to disregard ethics.

Once again, let's address the elephant in the room. Pride is the root of a savior complex. It is the core belief that a person possesses enough in them to save others from their problems. It is a belief that causes a person to step outside of their authentic role and assignment and usurp Christ's role as the savior.

One key element to defeating this level of pride is through supplication. From a biblical perspective, supplication is when a person pleads humbly for the power to accomplish a task. When leaders recognize that they are powerless and ineffective without Christ leading and guiding their actions, it allows them to operate without the driving urge to be the answer to everyone's problems.

The danger of pride is that it sneaks up on leaders who are unaware. While pride is obvious to others, the leader in bondage to pride's grip is often oblivious to their shortcomings. To spot pride, I suggest analyzing the areas of your life that compromise your authentic nature. For some, it can be found in the subtle manifestation of insecurity, in the inner desire to be accepted, applauded, and affirmed. In others, it can be found in the braggadocious desire to be front and center. In each case, pride causes the leader to behave in a manner that opposes their true nature.

Humpty Dumpty

Remember the nursery rhyme Humpty Dumpty? While this story is often told to children in grade school, it has profound significance for adult leaders. If you indulge me, I would like to conclude this chapter by pointing out a few observations that will cause you to see this story in a new light. The story goes as follows:

> *Humpty Dumpty sat on a wall,*
> *Humpty Dumpty had a great fall;*
> *All the king's horses and all the king's men*
> *Couldn't put Humpty together again.*
> *(Mother Goose)*

The first observation is that Humpty Dumpty was a person of importance despite his desire to be prominent, which led him to sit higher than he should have.

As a leader, it is important to recognize the intrusive thoughts of pride. These thoughts can integrate into a person's personality and drive them to believe they hold a more significant status than they actually do. Jesus warns against this in the parable of the guests. He states: "When you are invited to a wedding banquet, do not sit in the place of honor, in case someone more distinguished than you has been invited. Then the host who invited both of you will come and tell you, 'Give this man your seat.' And in humiliation, you will have to take the last place. For everyone who exalts himself will be humbled, and he who humbles himself will be exalted." Luke 14:8-11" Inevitably, Humpty's desire to sit high would lead to his public embarrassment.

Humpty, often portrayed as an egg by illustrators, had a body too fragile for his seat placement. But the real question observers should ask is what would cause him to sit so high with such a delicate body? Anyone analyzing Humpty Dumpty's position would notice that the ground would be the safest place for his egg-shelled body. Instead, his high seat on the wall led him to his demise. Ultimately, where he ended up after the fall was exactly where he should have been in the first place: the ground. The Bible states: "Pride goes before destruction, and a haughty spirit before a fall. It is better to be of lowly spirit with the poor than to divide the spoil with the proud" (Proverbs 16:18-19 ESV).

Leaders must realize that no matter the bravado, hyperinflating, or even underinflating, self-importance is simply a mask that will eventually be pulled off, uncovering the true nature of one's character. In Humpty's case, his desire to be prominent caused him to miss out on the fact that he was important long before his self-imposed seat on the wall. This is revealed in the depiction of those who came to his aid. It wasn't ordinary people who showed up to rescue him but those sent by royal decree. As the king's horses and men came to piece him together, they did so because of his position and favor with the king.

One reading this must realize that the results of pride can be devastating, crushing a person in ways that will lead them never to recover fully. While this story is illusory, its implication for those seeking to lead authentically is of the utmost importance. When leaders engage in behaviors influenced by pride, they eventually come to a place where they are face-to-face with reality. A reality in which the scars from their fall imprint themselves into the fabric of their character. For some, these scars cause them to live life with a humbler perspective, while others double down deeper into the pit of their ego.

The key takeaway from this story for anyone seeking to lead from a place of authenticity is to stay grounded in Christ. When a leader is securely positioned on the floor, there is no place left for them to fall. Rather than compromising authenticity, strong leaders must challenge themselves to stay keenly aware of their status, not thinking of themselves more highly or less than their actual designation in life. A balance swinging toward either side indicates that the assassin called Pride is lurking nearby.

SECTION II:

RELIEVING THE PRESSURE

FOUR
SHIFTING THE PRESSURE

Come to me, all who labor and are heavily laden, and I will give you rest. Take my yoke upon you, and learn from me, for I am gentle and lowly in heart, and you will find rest for your souls. For my yoke is easy, and my burden is light." (Matthew 11:28-30 ESV)

Picture this: our bodies are like walking stories, each scar a sentence, every ache a paragraph of some deeper narrative. When I stepped into the chiropractor's office, I didn't realize that I was about to revisit a chapter of my life I'd previously glossed over.

As I arrived for my first assessment, the doctor used a tool to examine the strain in my back. She decoded tensions in my body like they were morse code. But the plot thickened when she brought out the X-rays. "Alan," she said, with a tone of discovery, "it looks like you had quite the fall once." She was spot on—I had a skateboarding accident as a teen that I hadn't given a second thought until she pointed out the evidence right there on my tailbone.

But it was the next revelation that truly got me. She pointed to the X-ray of my neck, explaining how its unusual curve wasn't just physical. It was a shadow of a time when fear and anxiety had a vice-like grip on me. It made sense. There were years when fear was like a constant, uninvited companion.

Hearing the chiropractor link my spine's condition to my past fears was a silent thunderclap of realization. How do we fix this? I asked, half expecting a simple solution. Her answer was profound—many chiropractors believe our bodies have an innate, God-given ability to self-heal when our spine is in proper alignment. She explained that when the spine is out of alignment, the body cannot receive the correct signals from the brain to heal. She suggested that the right amount of pressure applied to my spine would shift my bones back in place so that I could find my way back to health.

But this idea of pressure is not just a physical therapy thing. It's everywhere. Look at the news; nations seem to be teetering on the brink of chaos. Our personal lives feel like pressure cookers too, full to the brim with daily stresses from all the roles we play.

Here's the thing, though: pressure isn't just a force that compresses; it's also a transformative power. Like grapes into wine, olives into oil, and coal into diamonds, pressure is an agent of change. It's easy to get lost in feeling squeezed and forget the new shapes we're forming into. It's about perspective, seeing not just the force bearing down on us but also the potential beauty it's creating within us. It's about embracing the pressure, not as an enemy but as a challenging friend, guiding us through becoming something precious, something stronger.

The pull to fit in, to become one with the crowd, is as common to us as the air we breathe. We are players on a stage where societal trends and public opinion often write the script. In today's world, the weight of 'cancel culture' looms like a judge, ready to bang the gavel at the slightest step outside the lines of social acceptance. It's a world where standing up can mean standing alone, where taking a stance against the grain may make you push off the stage entirely.

For those on the journey to authentic leadership, this pressure is like a gale force wind, threatening to blow them off course. In the professional arena, the race to climb the ladder, be seen, and be famous often pushes individuals to wear masks that don't fit their true faces. Imagine the strain of acting a part every day that's not written for you. It's like wearing a shoe two sizes too small; it may look great, but behind the scenes, it pinches!

Yet, the secret to staying on your feet during gale-force winds is not bending like a reed but standing firm like an oak with roots of authenticity. It's about finding the light that makes you shine, no matter the stage. This doesn't mean resisting the ability to adapt or grow; rather, it's about ensuring the growth is true to your inner self.

Consider an actor tasked with a role that goes completely against their nature. They may give a stunning performance, but each act drains more and more out of them. This is the crux of burnout, a candle burning at both ends and from the inside out. The task, then, is not to mold yourself into the character the world expects but to write your role, to turn your truth into your public performance. In this way, an authentic leader crafts their legacy, not in the echoes of applause for a part well played, but in the bold and authentic voice of their own story, being bravely told through their life.

Conclusion

Consider the daily challenge of fitting in, the way we alter ourselves to gain others' approval. This balancing act can feel like a daily performance. Yet, it's important to realize that the facades we present for acceptance are often showcased for those who may never truly appreciate our genuine selves. Have you ever thought that perhaps your brightest moments happen not when you conform to others' expectations but when you dare to be uniquely yourself?

Embrace the idea of being different, like a square peg that won't fit into a world of round holes. There is immense value in recognizing and honoring your unique role in life. This book cannot overstate this point: You are the uniquely designed craftsmanship of an all-knowing, all-powerful, and ever-present God. A God who created only one of you to exist. In all of creation, there will never be another you. You were designed to inspire, empower, create, design, influence, and do the handiwork of God. Your presence is not a random event but a deliberate act of creation, a unique aspect of a larger design. When you live in sync with who God created you to be, you follow a path designed just for you, leading to the truest form of fulfillment.

As a leader entrusted with inspiring others, it is also crucial to recognize that God's purpose and plan extend to those under your guidance. Your followers' backgrounds, cultural influences, ideologies, ethnic identities, strengths, and weaknesses all play an important role in shaping their contributions to your team's success. When a leader grasps an understanding beyond the talents and skillsets of those around them, it equips them with a deeper understanding of how to inspire their followers towards success both on a personal and professional level.

In a meeting with a client facing resistance from a local committee, I was struck by the contrast between my client, a hardworking baby boomer with conservative values, and a young, progressive mayor. Despite their differences, I recalled a valuable lesson from a Gen Z-focused seminar led by Dr. James Choung at Intervarsity Christian Fellowship. It highlighted the unique spiritual perspective at the heart of each generation: Boomers seek truth and hard evidence; Gen X values authentic experiences; Millennials pursue justice; and Gen Z appreciates beauty and aesthetics.

With this insight, I transformed my client's data-centric proposal into one aligned with the mayor's commitment to societal good. This approach not only facilitated the project's approval, but also established a successful program that reflected the genuine motivations of both parties, yielding lasting benefits for the client and the community.

In the overarching story of our lives, every challenge and pressure we encounter serves not as an obstacle but as a tool that sculpts us into the remarkable individuals we are meant to be. We must remain true to ourselves as we navigate the turbulence of opinion and societal expectations. Our journey's narrative is not scripted by conformity. It is painted with bold strokes of individuality guided and intentionally placed in our lives by God.

As we conclude this chapter, remember that you are a creation meticulously shaped with purpose and boundless potential. As a leader, your calling is not to fade into the background noise of the world but to stand out as a testament to the brilliance of your Creator.

May the challenges you face be seen as an influence shaping you into your authentic self. Of perceiving each day as a struggle to conform, may you embrace it as an opportunity to stand confidently in your purpose. May your leadership serve as a guiding light, inspiring others to recognize their worth within the grand design of God's master plan.

FIVE

THE PRESSURE FOR PEACE AND FREEDOM

"Peace, I leave with you; my peace I give to you. Not as the world gives do I give to you. Let not your hearts be troubled, neither let them be afraid." (John 14:27 ESV)

I couldn't believe it. It was as if I was reading the news in a state of alarm. The words gripped my eyes like a vice, squeezing out tears at the proclamation that our beloved state representative had died in a car accident because of a drunk driver. He wasn't just any government official but a beloved pillar in our community. It would be months later that news would circulate regarding levels of marijuana and alcohol in his system. While the temptation to engage in critiquing the event arose, I avoided the subject, knowing that the larger issue at hand was not the accident but the substance abuse behind it. My strongest concern was the very pressures that would cause a person to seek comfort in substances that only temporarily relieve the burden that leaders face. This desperation for relief is a cry for peace amidst the chaos that sometimes accompanies leadership.

For many, peace is an enigma, a mist, a vapor that fleetingly escapes the hand's grasp. In theory, it is a promise that provides hope but feels complex in the practical elements of life. In writing this chapter, I hope to assure you that God's design for the life of a leader was never meant to be one of burden and pressure. Instead, our lives were designed in such a way that would reflect the Kingdom of God.

Theologians summarize this kingdom and its elements in just one word: peace.

I dare say that peace is one of the boundaries that separate the Kingdom of God from the kingdoms of this world. When Adam was molded from the dust of the earth, he was set in the Garden of Eden as a watchman. His job and function was to set order by naming the animals and maintaining the garden. In essence, God positioned Adam as a leader; however, when sin entered the world, peace was disrupted, and the consequences were dire. The result was death and separation from the very presence of God, who walked with Adam in the cool of the day.

Sin has a way of perverting our peace. It blinds our eyes to the reality that God's design for our lives is to experience the peace of His kingdom. We can be assured of this because of the promises found in Scripture. Please pay attention to Isaiah's prophetic decree regarding the promised Messiah: For to us, a child is born, to us, a son is given, and the government will be on his shoulders. And he will be called Wonderful Counselor, Mighty God, Everlasting Father, Prince of Peace. When we dig into this promise, we notice that the names associated with the Messiah in this passage signify His leadership. He is the Wonderful Counselor advising and influencing His people through the empowerment of the Holy Spirit. He is the Mighty God victorious in battle that crushes the enemy, and He is the Prince of Peace, reconciling a broken world and broken people to a place of wholeness. Christ's role in entering the world as the Messiah was to be the source that brought mankind back into a place of peace.

While the promise of peace is enough to be assured of God's intent for our lives, we would be remiss if we did not briefly look at the establishment and fulfillment of these Old Testament promises and what they mean for our lives as leaders in the Kingdom of God. To do this, we will start with the narrative of Christ's birth.

On the night Christ was born, an announcement was proclaimed that altered the course of history. Luke details it in his writing:

> Then the angel said to them, "Do not be afraid, for behold, I bring you good tidings of great joy which will be to all people. For there is born to you this day in the city of David a Savior, who is Christ the Lord. And this will be the sign to you: You will find a Babe wrapped in swaddling cloths, lying in a manger." And suddenly there was with the angel a multitude of the heavenly host praising God and saying: "Glory to God in the highest, And on earth peace, goodwill toward men!" (Luke 2:9-14 NKJV)

This announcement is revelatory! It not only details the arrival of the promised Messiah, but it is a decree that the peace and goodwill God established in the Garden of Eden is now restored on earth through Christ's birth.

As we study the life of Jesus, it is apparent that His preaching and demonstration of casting out devils, performing miracles, and healing the sick was a manifestation of the Kingdom. When reading through the Gospels, you will notice that Jesus did not preach a message of salvation. Instead, we find that the Gospel Jesus preached was the Gospel of the Kingdom, a manifestation of peace. When peace was established, disease was uprooted, demons were cast out, lepers were healed, the blind began to see, and the lame began to leap. When these demonstrations occurred, the masses would show up to receive a measure of peace through the manifestation of the Kingdom of God in their lives.

The lifestyle of an authentic leader should be one that reflects the peace of God. It is a lifestyle that brings peace through conflict resolution, serving the needs of others, training, development, empowerment, and creating a sense of self-efficacy among followers. Far too often, I ask people who desire wealth the motive behind their ambition, only to receive a self-motivated answer. If your desire to take on a venture is solely motivated by money, power, and influence, your priorities are out of order. Instead, seek to use your business endeavor or idea to bring peace and enrich the lives of those you serve first. In doing this, you will find greater success in your work. You will also find a new and profound revelation of freedom.

The Revelation of Freedom

Woven in the threads of American history is the story of the prolific freedom fighter Harriet Tubman. For those unfamiliar with her story, Tubman's narrative is not merely a chapter in the pages of history but a saga that reshaped the very fabric of a nation. When you dive deeper into the story of this mighty woman, you find that her life was a chronicle of bravery, a series of acts so audacious that they would seem fictitious were they not anchored in the foundations of history. She was not just a fugitive from the chains of slavery; she was an orchestrator of emancipation, a general in the battle against enslavement, and a prophetess of freedom.

I often wonder how a woman born into a system of stark contrasts where the color of her skin dictated the course of her life dared to believe in the possibility of freedom. In the face of adversity, the penalty of death, dismemberment, and public humiliation, Tubman courageously decided that she would not be a statistic in a system that was considered status quo for the majority of her race in the United States.

Her journey to freedom was sparked not by a singular decision to flee but by a profound revelation, an epiphany that blossomed in the depths of her soul. When she learned of her master's intent to sell her, as he had sold her sisters before her, something within Harriet awakened. The unwavering conviction was that she would not share the same fate as those before her, nor would she remain passive toward the trade of human lives.

In Harriet Tubman, we witness the story of a heroic leader who dared to live out the revelation of freedom that existed in her mind. It was a revelation that led her to believe that beyond the walls of enslavement, there was more for her.

In the quest for authentic leadership, there comes a pivotal point where a leader must decide to step out of the boxes considered normal. Far too often, I engage people who refuse to travel beyond the borders of their city, people who are bound by tradition, religiosity, and a familiarity that stifles innovation. I find that asking people with this mindset to think, believe, and try things differently is akin to a dentist pulling their teeth out without the numbing effects of anesthesia.

As a minority, I often consider the hardships of generational poverty, systemic illiteracy, and the lack of resources that this way of thinking has elicited in my community. I often leave the series of thoughts that run through my mind by reflecting on one of Harriet Tubman's famous quotes where she profoundly writes:

"I freed a thousand slaves, and I would have freed a thousand more if they only knew they were slaves." Harriet Tubman

For Tubman, the mindset of slavery was much worse than the brutality of physical enslavement. Her desire, depicted in how she lived her life, was fueled by a burning passion to lead others to freedom. Tubman's narrative sheds a profound lesson for the authentic leader who may struggle with breaking free from upbringing and social status limitations. The lesson is that when leaders encounter a revelation of freedom for themselves, they internalize the mission to provoke a life of freedom in their followers.

When employed, Tubman's mindset threatens autocratic and bottom-line driven leaders as their ambitions are primarily focused on achieving goals and not the betterment and wellbeing of their followers. On the contrary, authentic leadership progresses beyond personal development and ventures into the development of those the leader influences into action. A leader's greatest success can be measured by how they assist others in attaining a revelation of freedom for themselves.

Conclusion

In closing this chapter, I invite you to examine the areas of your life that lack peace and freedom and surrender them to Christ. The absence of peace that you may be experiencing could indicate an unoccupied area by the Kingdom of God. It is important to realize that Jesus has us positioned to be peacemakers, bettering the lives of those around us through enforcing His kingdom. Peace, by definition, involves freedom, and the definition of freedom requires elements of peace. The overarching unifier of these two words exists on the premise that limitations must be broken.

When confronted with the opportunity to venture beyond life's walls and borders, I challenge you to become your ancestor's wildest dreams. Do in your life what seemed impossible to those who came before you. I implore you to dream what has never been dreamed, fly what has never been flown, and live beyond expectation. The truest form of your authenticity depends on it.

SIX

RELEASING THE PRESSURE OF COMPARISON

Not that we dare to classify or compare ourselves with some of those who are commending themselves. But when they measure themselves by one another and compare themselves with one another, they are without understanding. (2 Corinthians 10:12 ESV)

In the past, my days were often consumed with examining the lives of extraordinary faith figures. I spent hours on end reading my Bible and immersing myself in the teachings and sermons of influential leaders such as Smith Wigglesworth, Kathryn Kuhlman, and A.A. Allen, as well as numerous modern-day television preachers. My fresh perspective as a recent Christian convert brought an intense curiosity about how God could remarkably transform seemingly ordinary people into conduits for His extraordinary work. These stories of faith heightened my own, yet they also kindled a deep yearning to mirror their spiritual fervor and miraculous works. The ambition to emulate Wigglesworth's steadfast faith, Kuhlman's supernatural ministry, or the healing power of Rev. Allen was overshadowed by an underlying sentiment encompassed in just one word: fear.

For some, the idea of fear is overt, like a phobia that paralyzes a person taking on a challenge. I find it interesting how walking across a bridge, climbing a high ladder, or seeing a spider can bring some of the most formidable people to a standstill. Then there's the more insidious kind of fear, the kind I'm familiar with. This sort operates under the radar, a hidden but growing belief that lies in wait, ready to ambush at the worst possible time.

This fear came to light while I was being trained in ministry when my pastor requested that I preach a short sermon the week after Thanksgiving. I threw myself into the preparation, prayed, and fasted mightily, but somewhere along the way, my focus shifted. When it was time to speak, I realized I was trying to echo the faith leaders I admired rather than being true to myself. In hindsight, that sermon wasn't my finest hour. It was an earnest but awkward effort, shaped by the worry that my voice wouldn't be enough.

This moment of youthful inexperience isn't unique to me; I've since learned that even seasoned leaders can find themselves in this trap of comparison. Nowadays, the relentless stream of social media and the rapid evolution of technology can make it feel like we're always a step behind. With every scroll through trending hashtags and viral videos, it's easy to fall into the cycle of imitation, all while losing bits of our authentic selves.

In this chapter, I will highlight ways to diffuse the pressure of comparison that creeps up and sabotages even the best leaders. You will grow and thrive as an authentic leader by incorporating a strong vision for where you are leading others and a deep understanding of those under your leadership.

Strong Leaders Require Strong Vision

In the quest for authenticity, a leader's vision becomes the compass that empowers them to lead. The common denominator of great leaders can be found in their passion and endurance to press toward a greater vision. From a leadership perspective, vision is the framework for every decision-making process. At its best, vision is a vivid and detailed depiction of an un-accomplishable endeavor. The ability to envision something that stretches beyond our time here on Earth is what separates a strong leader from the pack. Your vision should be a vast dream that remains unfinished not just in your lifetime but even in those who continue to follow your plan. Why? It is simply because it ensures that you and your followers always reach for more, for something beyond the horizon.

Take, for example, the enduring directive found in the Great Commission in Matthew 28:19-20. It isn't just a task to complete; it's a lifelong mission that transcends generations: to spread teachings, to baptize, to guide in obedience, all in the vision of advancing the kingdom of God. In essence, all vision statements should possess a boundless endeavor strongly rooted in passion, grounded in reality, and succinct enough to memorize. A vision statement such as this ensures that those who follow it will be able to hone its passion and recite it on command. A true leader doesn't just provide a roadmap; they light a fire in the hearts of others, empowering them to take up the mission and weave it into their very purpose. Leadership is about movement, inspiring action, and cultivating the seeds of a vision that will grow and flourish long after we're gone.

In this space, true leaders emerge into their God-given calling. They are those touched by the hand of God, ready to champion a heavenly cause in an authentic manner. These leaders burst onto the scene, not just in the church but in places beyond the confines of the pulpit and the steeple. They are the bold, innovative weirdos that God has marked to make an authentic impact in the world around them. They are unafraid to take kingdom principles and vision into the marketplace, educational sectors, media, and entertainment fields. They run in purpose, on purpose, and through purpose, and shake the Earth with a kingdom-minded vision.

This was the case with an organization I helped to lead several years ago. Their vision was solid, memorable, and un-accomplishable. It was to educate, equip, and edify all young men and women to be leaders in the community. Was it possible that ALL young men and women involved in our program would become leaders? The answer is no, but it gave us something to continuously strive for in our ministry. For years, we ran a leadership academy providing services to advance youth in the areas of public speaking, financial literacy, graphic design, social media etiquette, and academic success. While some time has passed since our last youth academy, I still encounter many young faces who have participated in our programming, practicing the very lessons and kingdom principles we instilled in them so long ago.

Possessing a strong vision serves as both a compass and a shield for a leader, ensuring that their actions are not just random strokes but deliberate steps towards an authentic purpose. It is a boundary set up to protect the destiny of a person or an organization. When leaders hone the skill of understanding and adhering to vision, they move more intentionally. Such focused leadership is not only efficient, but has the power to inspire and galvanize others toward a shared objective.

Incorporating a strong vision statement for your life, family, and organizational culture is not just strategic; it's a way of infusing purpose into every facet of your existence. It is about moving with conviction, where each decision and each action aligns with the broader narrative you wish to write for yourself and those you lead.

If you are in a place where you are struggling to figure out the next step in life or what God has in store for you, take a moment to surrender your future to God. While it may seem cliché, I believe God's power will assist you in this newly surrendered space to craft a vision anchored in Christ and rooted in the unique way He created you.

Authentic Leaders Know, Grow, and Throw

Imagine standing at the forefront of a path that stretches far beyond the horizon. It's the path of leadership, and as you look back, you see the faces of those who have followed you and those whose journeys you've shaped. I've often pondered a profound truth that resonated deeply as I turned the pages of my Bible. Jesus said, "Truly, truly, I say to you, whoever believes in me will also do the works that I do; and greater works than these will he do because I am going to the Father." (John 14:12 ESV). At first, this statement left me in a whirlwind of thought. How could we, with our finite capabilities, exceed the works of Jesus Himself? But then it dawned on me that the essence of monumental leadership is not about the leader. It's about the legacy, the generational impact that continues to ripple out long after we've passed the baton.

The Bible doesn't just tell us about leadership; it shows us. We witness Elijah passing his mantle to Elisha, Jesus empowering His disciples with the Holy Spirit, and Paul nurturing future pillars of faith like Timothy. They didn't just fill shoes; they expanded the footprint.

And here's the crux: Leadership is not about cloning ourselves in others. It's about nurturing the distinct, God-given potential within each person. We must resist the urge to shape others into our image. Instead, we should encourage them to fully discover and inhabit their unique callings.

You may wonder how it is possible to lead others in ways that nurture their unique potential. If so, look no further than the Bible. In the book of Matthew, Jesus is confronted by men from Capernaum requesting that he pay taxes. His reply was to send Peter out to catch a fish with a coin in its mouth. When Peter catches this fish, the coin is enough to cover both Peter's and Jesus' taxes. The lesson in this narrative can be found in how Jesus knew, grew, and threw Peter into this assignment.

Knowing, growing, and throwing is the kind of leadership that doesn't just instruct but transforms. From Peter's example, we can see the profound impact of authenticity in servant leadership, a concept modeled perfectly by Jesus. It isn't just about being in charge; it's about being present, about fostering a space where everyone feels seen, heard, and inspired to grow.

If you recall, Peter was a skilled fisherman, and Jesus recognized this talent. He didn't send Peter out to craft materials out of wood because it was not his skill set. Instead, He used Peter powerfully in a way that applied to his trade. If you examine this closely, you will see that Jesus "knew" Peter's talents, "grew" Peter to a level of maturity and obedience, and "threw" him into a mutually beneficial opportunity. A bottom-line-driven leader's focus is to accomplish the task at hand, but a servant leader seeks to reap results while empowering their followers to succeed.

Now, let's look deeper at knowing, growing, and throwing.

Knowing- "Knowing" in leadership means truly connecting with the people you lead. It's about more than just their resumes; it's about their dreams, challenges, and lives. Imagine having real conversations where you listen more than you speak and learn about the hopes that kindle in their hearts and the hurdles they face. That's how you start to build a team that's efficient, truly cohesive, and synergistic.

Growing- Consider how Jesus prepared His disciples for the tasks and path ahead. In the same way, we should be looking to nurture our team's talents. Offer them the tools to sharpen their skills and the opportunities to explore new ones. Whether through further education, diverse training, or leadership courses, commit to helping your team members flourish in every aspect of their lives.

Throwing- While it might seem odd, it is about giving people the chance to shine. It's delegating with trust, sending them out as Jesus did with His disciples, to make a difference in their own right. It's saying, "I believe in you. Now go show the world what you're capable of." This is how we encourage innovation and a sense of ownership that can light up a workplace.

We need to move beyond the old pyramids of hierarchy to embed these practices into the DNA of our lives and organizations. This will help create an ecosystem where service to one another is encouraged and celebrated. An environment where humility, patience, and genuine care for each other's growth are honored as core values. Doing so will transform our organizations and elevate them to places where every individual is encouraged to reach their fullest potential and achieve more than they ever thought possible.

The mark of a great leader is someone who plants trees under whose shade they may never sit. When this is accomplished, they will find that their legacy is not just a path that leads others to walk in their footsteps, but a vast network of trails blazed by those who learned to lead in their own right.

My message to you, as leaders, is this: strive to be the ones who light the fires of innovation and passion in those who follow. Create spaces where they can grow, challenge them to think differently, and equip them with the courage to venture into new territories. This is how we do greater works, not by our hands alone, but by empowering many hands to carry on the mission with their distinct touch.

SEVEN
UNLEASHING YOUR INNER WEIRDO

*Your hands made me and formed me; give me the understanding to
learn your commands.
May those who fear you rejoice when they see me, for I have put
my hope in your word.*
(Psalm 119:73-74 NIV)

The whole experience was quite surreal. I had the
honor of being invited to deliver a sermon in the town
where I grew up, and as the event drew closer, my
excitement swelled. Yet, the second I stepped into the church
—a place I'd never visited despite being invited to speak—I
sensed a shift. Welcomed and directed to wait in the pastor's
office, I was surprised to learn the pastor was on vacation.
Being handed the pulpit on a Sunday was unexpected
without meeting the pastor.

In the office, I encountered a young woman from the
media team. I asked if she could display a slide during my
talk, but she insisted on the pastor's approval. It struck me as
peculiar, but respecting the host church's practices was

something I had been taught, so I accepted it as their custom. Little did I know that the following events would forever imprint on my memory.

In preparation, I had fasted for two weeks, following divine guidance, and had meticulously penned my sermon. When it came time, I preached passionately from Jeremiah, with my wife, among the congregation. The response was overwhelmingly positive. I had the go-ahead to minister post-sermon, so I began to lay hands and prophesy, receiving confirmations at every turn. The Holy Spirit's presence was palpable until I was cut off by an elder, phone in hand, through which the pastor's voice accused me of being a false prophet. The room plunged into chaos, with gasps and objections, as the pastor on the call declared my message untrue and abruptly ended the service.

I was stunned, my heart sinking as I grappled with what had just occurred. I took a seat to maintain harmony, though confusion whirled within me. Congregation members approached me with offerings, reassuring me there must have been some mistake. I was determined to seek clarity on this unexpected accusation.

The pastor phoned me three days later, starting the conversation with hostility. When I pressed for specifics about the alleged falsity in my sermon, he conceded there was none; it was a matter of broken protocol, a protocol that I wasn't even aware of.

This ordeal almost deterred me from my calling. I felt a tumult of emotions: betrayal, fury, sorrow, all leading to utter weariness. I wept until my resolve was as stained as my cheeks, fearing I'd never find closure or justice with that pastor. But in that low moment, divine encouragement came. God gave me an acronym that allowed me to realize that what I went through did not have the power to break me, but that it would make me a more resilient young minister. God told me to S.I.T., standing for 'Still In Training.' It was a revelation, reshaping my perspective on life. Each life lesson was a training ground that sharpened me like a sword being prepared for battle.

Leadership is often tested through hardships, be it legal threats, public humiliation, or slander. Despite the temptation to retreat, the resolve to persevere often prevails. I've faced many such trials, enough to make me want to hide away and weep. Yet, I've gleaned invaluable lessons from these experiences. Lessons I'm eager to share in the final chapter of this guide to authentic leadership.

Figure out Who You Are

One of my toughest challenges was discovering my life's purpose and learning to live it out. As a newcomer to Christianity, the church was abuzz with many eager to guide my spiritual journey. My fervor and eagerness for the Word were palpable. It was then that figures like my pastor and mother in law invested in me, developing me in a way that I could encounter God personally. However, I also met people who aimed to mold me into their replicas, echoing the familiar refrains of church tradition and ritual. Thankfully, even in my spiritual infancy, I could sense that some teachings didn't align with God's intentions for me.

My journey to understanding my purpose became clearer when I embraced personality tests. These assessments, like Strength Finders, Myers-Briggs, Enneagram, and DISC, are instrumental in shining a light on strengths and areas for development, particularly in leadership.

The APEST test is beneficial in Christian faith settings as it identifies the strongest gifts concerning a leader's fivefold ministry role. Although the theology behind the five-fold ministry can spark debate, I encourage leaders to draw parallels between the ministry roles in Ephesians 4:11 and the standard roles in most businesses.

Consider this: someone with the gift of an Apostle often acts similarly to a CEO, setting visions for various parts of an organization and ensuring their realization. A Prophet mirrors a Vice President, guiding the company toward its mission's completion. An Evangelist is akin to a Marketing and Outreach Director, promoting what the company provides. A Pastor, resembling a Human Resources expert, maintains organizational well-being. Lastly, a Teacher is comparable to a Training and Development Director, ensuring the team is well-prepared for their tasks.

It's essential to recognize that skills from religious service can be applied in the business world. Serving in a religious capacity can teach you how to conduct meetings, manage business activities, mentor, lead, and advise. Recognizing and applying these skills in religious and professional settings is important in learning your authentic place in the world.

Understand the Power of N.O.W.

Growing up, I learned the valuable lesson of hard work. I spent my summers working at a small screw machine shop alongside my grandfather. Day after day, I would leave, wreaking from the oil smell. I would jokingly suggest that child labor laws didn't apply to my family as I worked countless amounts of time for a whopping $3.00 an hour.

Come to think about it, I've always worked and watched my parents' work.

At age 25, I found myself living in Connecticut; I had a job that my family was proud of. Many of them had worked as state employees, and they saw this as a continuation of a legacy. But the reality was far from the ideal they pictured. I wasn't hired for my skills or talents but rather to fill a routine role. Most of my shifts were during the evenings, and my primary responsibility was to care for developmentally disabled adults. This often involved challenging tasks that were both physically and emotionally demanding.

While I had deep affection for my clients, the job took a toll on me. Over the years, I realized I needed to grow or learn. I felt stuck. The realization that I was losing myself in this role became stronger daily. I had to make a change.

Deciding to leave was challenging. People advised against it, saying it was a secure job, especially since I didn't have a college degree or a strong academic background. But, I believed in myself and my potential. I was willing to take the risk to find a job that resonated with who I truly was.

As I share my story, I recognize that many might be in a similar situation, feeling stuck in jobs that don't align with their aspirations. It's crucial to understand that fulfilling roles not aligned with your passions, skills, talents, and ambitions is not only a waste of your time but also a waste for others. Even reading this statement may provoke a feeling of helplessness and vulnerability. The fact is that many in society are working jobs to pay bills or support loved ones. The thought of making an immediate departure from that job to chase a dream would feel irresponsible; however, this way of thinking has the potential to create cycles that keep people stuck. I am not advocating for you to abandon taking care of your responsibilities. I am stating that you must learn to maximize your N.O.W. to move into an authentic lifestyle.

I want to share three key strategies for maximizing your present opportunities. Embrace these principles, and you'll transition from passively experiencing life to actively shaping your destiny. These strategies were pivotal in my journey from being a 25-year-old adult care provider to achieving academic honors throughout my collegiate career, preaching internationally, launching various enterprises, leading on several executive boards, and managing a historic project on a $100 million property, all within a decade. The acronym "N.O.W." stands for "No Opportunity Wasted, No One is Worthless, and You Only Need One Win." These are fundamental principles you must grasp to begin leading authentically.

No Opportunity Wasted

Take some time to reflect on your abilities. Identify your strengths, passions, and skills that positively affect the people around you. Ask yourself: How often do I apply my abilities, enthusiasm, and influence at work, in my enterprise, and the community? If your job actively involves your core passions, that's commendable; however, for many, there must be a stark contrast between their passions and their work.

In a session with a successful businessman, I asked a pivotal question: How does one amass wealth? He explained it as a process where a person masters something valuable, earns from it, and repeats it consistently. What I grasped from the conversation was different from what he said, but the essence of it. I learned that there is immense value in learning your lane, staying in your lane, and making the most out of your lane. Remember the "grace bubble" from the previous chapter. That is your lane.

Life presents many opportunities; some seem scarce, while others seem boundless. I've met many people who believe lacking opportunity means they cannot accomplish their dreams. Despite abundant opportunities, I've also met others who are held back by feelings of inadequacy. To those feeling restricted, I encourage you to seek even the smallest occasions to use your talents, especially in service to others. Using your talents spurs authentic growth. I can confidently state from experience that "Your gift will make room for you." (Proverbs 18:16)

Your talent is the gift that can unlock doors that keep you from realizing your authentic potential. Knowing that your gift, no matter how large or small, will open doors and opportunities that were once closed off to you is critical. This is because the very essence of your gift is tied to what God has in store for your life.

For the people reading this book who might struggle with a deep sense of inadequacy, I urge you to step out on faith and trust God with the opportunities in front of you. I am not asking you to walk into an opportunity without vision; I am asking that you trust that God will aid you in fulfilling the assignment after you prayerfully consider the opportunities on your plate and how they relate to your calling, skill, core beliefs, and the impact you can make in that given field.

Whether the opportunity in front of you is small or large, it must be well-spent. Whenever you have the chance to practice the giftings and skills that are central to your calling, use them.

No One is Worthless

Let's start with the understanding that "N.O.W." is more than a moment in time—it's a mindset that stands for "No one is worthless," and yes, that most certainly includes you. Every one of us has faced moments where we felt like outsiders, where rejection stung sharply, where abandonment, mistreatment, and abuse may have darkened our doors and made us feel worthless. It's not about whether those things should have happened to us; it's about the lessons they taught us while we journeyed through them. Have you grasped them? It's important to remember that there's value in every experience. Each person you encounter has something to teach you. I once faced rejection from the same man who, years later, offered me an immensely more valuable opportunity. He didn't see my potential initially, but I did not let that deter me. When the second chance came, I was ready to seize it with everything I had.

Some of you might have walked into a journey needing to fully understand the importance of what it would mean for your future. You may feel that you squandered an opportunity to be great. If this is the case, I advise you not to stay stuck in the past, wallowing in what feels like failed potential. Instead, dive in and take full advantage of the next time an opportunity comes your way. The very person or organization that denied you may be vying and willing to pay for you to use your skills for them later on in life.

As an authentic leader, you must believe that your presence here is no accident. You are unique and irreplaceable in the vast tapestry of creation. Even cloning cannot replicate the intricate details of your personality, the perspective you bring that is shaped by your gender, culture, passions, and disposition. You are not merely a product of your generation; you contribute to its definition.

I emphatically include you in that decree when I affirm that no one is worthless. I sit in rooms filled with perplexed faces, wondering how I, a simple man, have earned my seat at the table. The answer is belief—a belief in purpose and belonging. You are destined to be in rooms filled with decision-makers, to initiate impactful change, to voice critical ideas, and to live out your parents' wildest aspirations. You are far from worthless; you, my friends, are beyond valuable.

Need One Win

Let me share something with you. In my line of work, I regularly converse with millionaires, and it might surprise you to learn that many of them live in ordinary homes, drive standard cars, and can easily blend into a crowd without betraying their wealth. What I find more interesting is that I get to witness these same individuals fail. Yet, despite these setbacks, they share a common thread of success. What is their secret? They view fear and failure as mere hurdles, not roadblocks. They embrace the possibility of failure because they understand it's part of the process and not a final result. They subscribe to the belief that they "Need Only One Win." That one substantial victory has the potential to overshadow numerous defeats.

The lesson here is clear: striving for perfection should not overshadow the pursuit of getting things done. No matter how devastating things may seem, one major victory is a greater accomplishment than a million losses. Persist daily, fueled by the knowledge that one breakthrough is all it takes. One win can take you to the next stop in your destiny.

Conclusion

In life's grand design, each experience, every aspect of our personalities, and the expression of our talents contribute to the masterpiece that makes up our unique existence. The story you read exemplifies the impact of embracing our individuality, a gift bestowed upon us with the power not only for personal fulfillment but also to enrich the world around us.

As you find yourself at the intersection of reflection and anticipation, I encourage you to recognize the weirdo within you. The one that stays hidden in an attempt to be embraced and accepted by others in ways that diminish authenticity. It is important to recognize that your calling, purpose, and destiny are not a one-size-fits-all garment, but they are custom-made and tailored to your being. As a potter shapes clay with intentionality and care, God has carefully molded and crafted you with distinct differences to create a harmonious blend of abilities, passions, and talents.

Embracing authenticity is not solely a journey of self-discovery, but an expedition marked by collaboration. It necessitates attuning ourselves to the frequency of God, listening attentively to those whispers in a still, small voice that beckons us toward realizing our potential. It calls upon us to be courageous to venture beyond the shores of conformity into waters where genuine self-expression thrives.

As this book draws to a close and your gaze shifts towards what lies ahead, remember that cultivating authenticity is a process that unfolds gradually over time.

I urge you not to let the fear of making mistakes or the pressure of meeting expectations discourage you. Your uniqueness is not something to be hidden but something to be celebrated and shared with others. Embracing your individuality is a mark that sets you apart in this world.

I pray this realization inspires you to explore ways to nurture the inner weirdo the world is waiting to see. May you pursue growth with the understanding that every step forward brings you closer to becoming the person you were purposed to be.

I encourage every reader who holds these words close to their heart: Rise and continue growing. Discover your God-given mission, embrace it fully, and lead others to transformation; one weirdo at a time.

ABOUT THE AUTHOR

Rev. Alan Marshall II is a visionary, strategist, and keynote speaker passionate about developing Millennial and Gen Z leaders. As the Founder and Managing Partner of Upward Solutions, Alan has led teams to secure multiple multi-million-dollar tax abatements and is known for designing a historic set-aside for minority contractors in Connecticut. As a  consultant, Alan has been instrumental in his work on projects that have provided a total economic impact of over $1.5 billion and secured millions in capital for minority contractors.

Alan is also a skilled public speaker who provides leadership development through conferences, workshops, and small group settings nationally and internationally. Holding a bachelor's degree in Christian Ministry, a master's in organizational leadership, and ordination as a Reverend, Alan merges his ministry and leadership skills to develop the next generation of leaders.

It is not an understatement to say that Alan loves to volunteer by leading and assisting in various ministry capacities. Alan has served as the Director of Communications on the Board of Directors at Connecticut Christian Academy, Vice President of Noble and Unique Generation, a Youth Leader at Shiloh Christian Church, Campus Minister at Wesleyan University, Interim Regional Black Campus Ministry Coordinator at Intervarsity Christian Fellowship and on multiple missions internationally.

9798224498505